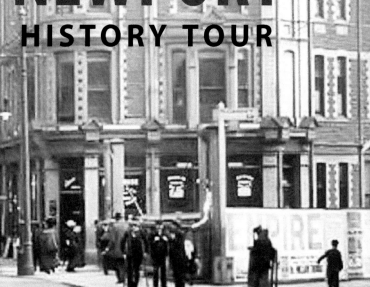

NEWPORT

HISTORY TOUR

*To my family and friends, and to those who see our
past as a guide to the future.*

First published 2019

Amberley Publishing
The Hill, Stroud,
Gloucestershire, GL5 4EP
www.amberley-books.com

Copyright © Jan Preece, 2019
Map contains Ordnance Survey data
© Crown copyright and database
right [2019]

The right of Jan Preece to be
identified as the Author of this work
has been asserted in accordance with
the Copyrights, Designs and Patents
Act 1988.

ISBN 978 1 4456 9292 0 (print)
ISBN 978 1 4456 9293 7 (ebook)

British Library Cataloguing in
Publication Data.
A catalogue record for this book is
available from the British Library.

Origination by Amberley Publishing.
Printed in Great Britain.

ACKNOWLEDGEMENTS

During the thirty years or more I have been involved in Pill Heritage many people have, with great kindness, shared their lives and their stories with me through the medium of photography and the written word. These people, many of whom do not wish to be mentioned, I thank profusely.

I have taken every effort to ascertain copyright and obtain permissions to use the enclosed images. In addition, I would like to especially thank those listed for their input and help: the late Terry Underwood; the late Cliff Knight; Duncan Brown; Malcom Beardmore; A. R. Adams; Jan Preece Picture Library and Heritage Collection; Don Carter, Gwent Family History; Doug Parker; Uskside Engineering Co.; Pill Heritage Centre; Mr Jim Oniel; and Jan Martin, Barnabus Arts Cente.

INTRODUCTION

In these days of 'here today, gone tomorrow' architecture, when everyday events become overblown news stories, often lacking truth and evidence, it is easy to think of history as something which has only happened in our own lifetime; something we can or have seen with our own eyes.

Without entering into the realms of history and prehistory, reliable and unreliable sources of evidence and carbon dating, I do feel that there is sufficient reliable information here in Newport to enable us to celebrate and feel part of the exciting journey of our city from the days of the Silurian tribes to the highly technical world into which we have all been plunged. The feeling of walking in another's footsteps, being in the hidden shadows of great buildings and in the spiritual company of the great men and women who were the elders of our city and community is compelling.

In writing *Newport History Tour*, I have revisited the past and have looked once more at images that I already know so well. I have endeavoured to see and portray events and subjects in a different light and present them accordingly, for the benefit of the community and for the visitor and those who join us from other parts.

KEY

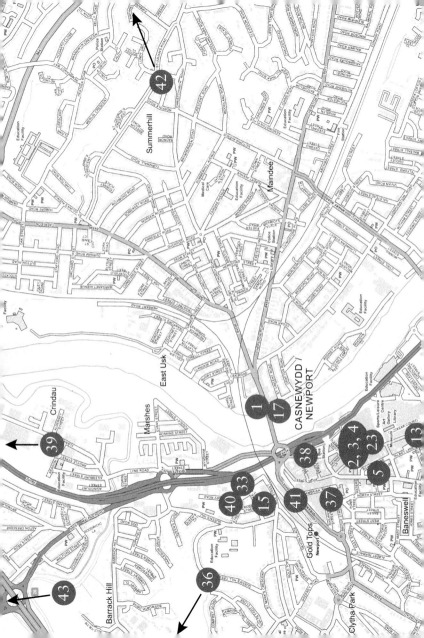

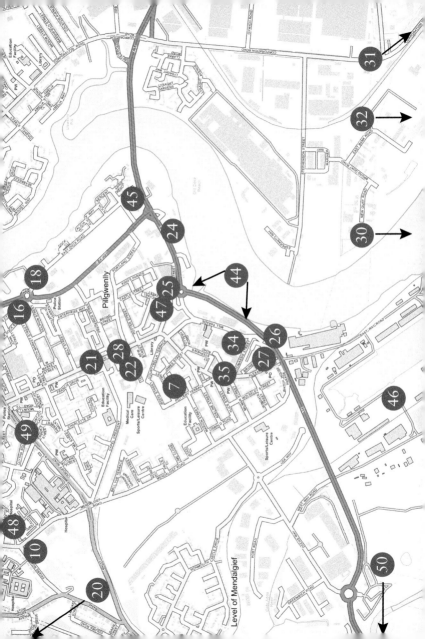

1. NEWPORT CASTLE

Newport Castle, robust with walls over 3 feet thick, is unique because in the centre it has a water gate. The only other one known is in the Tower of London, and it was through this gate that supplies, treasures and arms were brought in. The River Usk has always been used as a highway, as it was safer than travelling over land. The stone castle was built in the early Norman period and followed a wooden fort-type structure. At one point a moat surrounded the castle on the remaining three sides. Throughout its history it has been a brewery and a tannery and a store, but has now been heavily trimmed down for the new road.

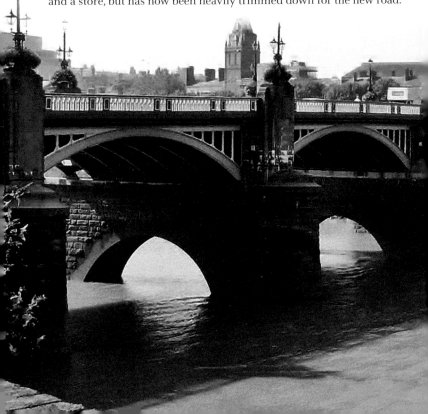

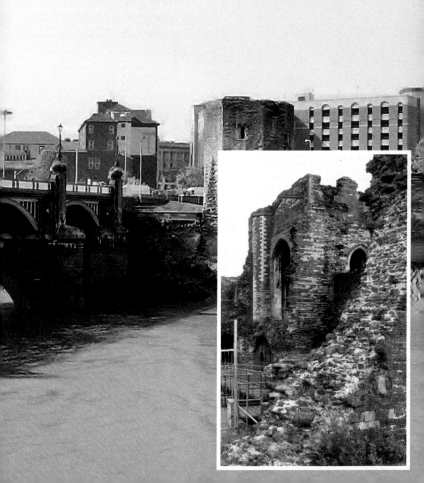

2. HIGH STREET

Newport has always enjoyed a good high street. In the early 1900s it was widened and more recently it was pedestrianised. Buses once terminated here before continuing on the second stage of their journey. WHSmiths stood on the site where McDonald's is now, on the left of picture, and the provision market has one of its entrances on the right-hand side. The original market hall was situated at the end of the street but vanished in the wake of major groundworks for the Monmouthshire Canal. *Inset*: Parades often came down High Street, giving the area a real sense of occasion.

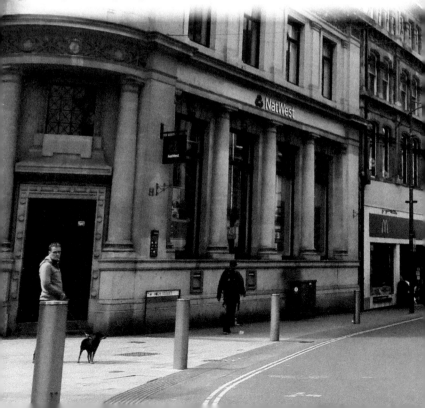

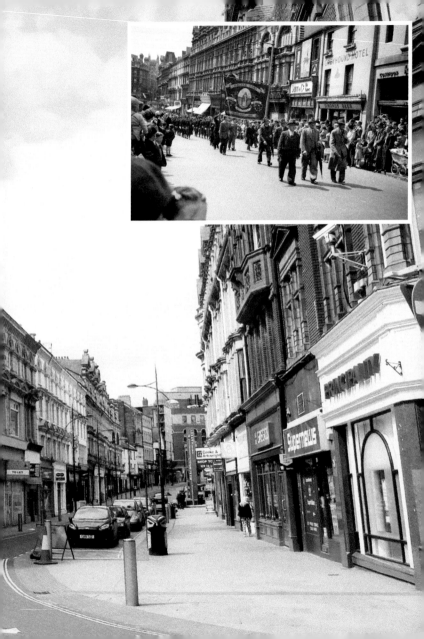

3. WESTGATE SQUARE

As the name suggests this was the West Gate, more or less. Time changes our environment so much that it is difficult to pinpoint the ancient when little physical evidence exists, and I am sure that the city's elders do not want an archeological dig in the middle of town. But this spot is a good one to just to sit and stare, raise your gaze above the garish plastic signage and soak in the elegance of a major Victorian town, known at one point as the most westerly port in England. This was also the banking heart of the old town, dating back to the late 1800s. And just look at the statues; they are so struck with the panorama that they haven't moved for years... *Inset*: Westgate Square, 1950.

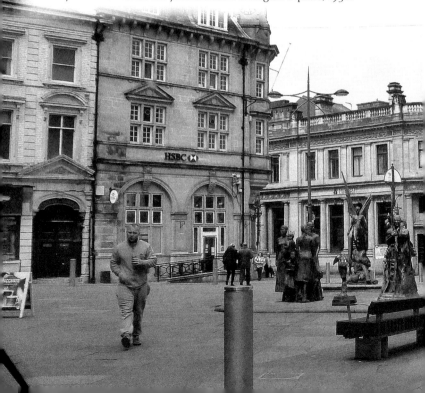

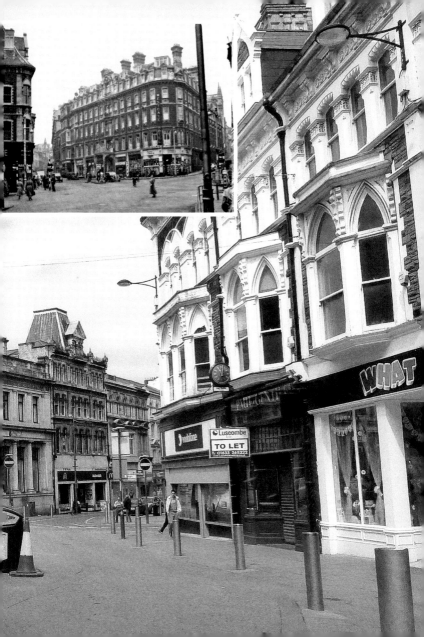

4. THE WESTGATE HOTEL

Still in the same location stands the Westgate Hotel. Its elegance suggests that it could have belonged to one of the great rail companies, but history here, on this spot, has a far greater significance. It was here that the Chartist uprising, led by John Frost in November 1839, took place, marking the start of a national uprising of Chartism. The hotel was occupied by regular soldiers who opened fire on the Chartists, killing more than twenty and injuring fifty more. This was to be the last uprising on British soil. This is not the original hotel, but parts remain and the bullet holes in the porch tell the tale. The Chartists gathered momentum and volume as they came down the valley – Stow Hill on the right of the hotel was the entrance route they had chosen. A small number had come from Newport, but the main body poured down the hill into the square, only to meet the armed soldiers.

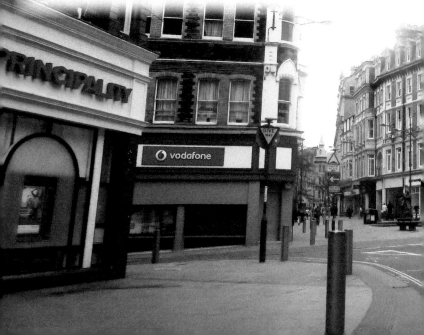

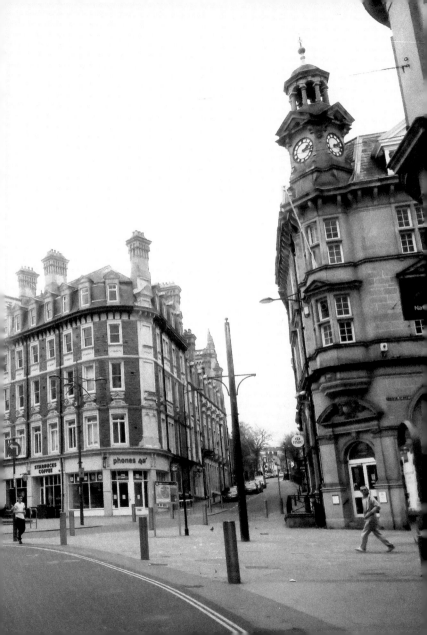

5. STOW HILL

Stow Hill was once a principle route out of Newport connecting the villages of Newport and Stow. Logically speaking it was hardly a connection as Stow was in viewing distance of Newport, which at that time was centered around the castle. It was not so much a tale of two cities but more of two markets, one being at the castle and the other at Stow. This leafy, relaxed area has much to say. St Mary's, the principle Catholic church, is just visible through the trees. On the same side, a little further along, was once the drill hall of the Monmouthshire Regiment. Havelock Street Presbyterian Church (left, out of view) is synonymous with the Boys' Brigade, being the first company in Newport and also in Wales, established in 1887.

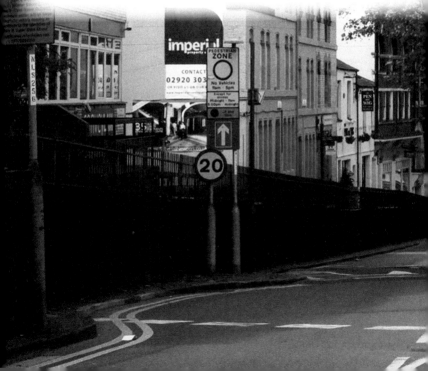

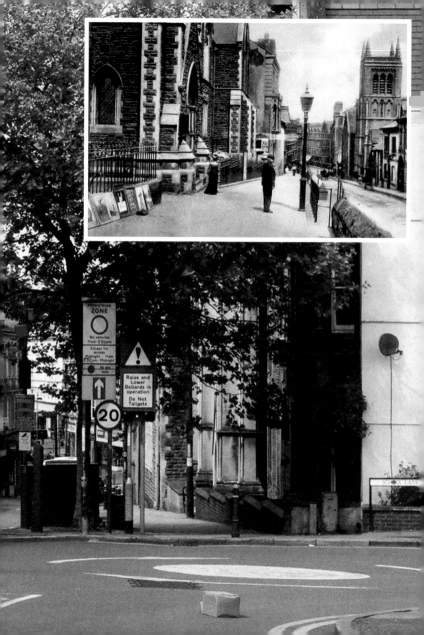

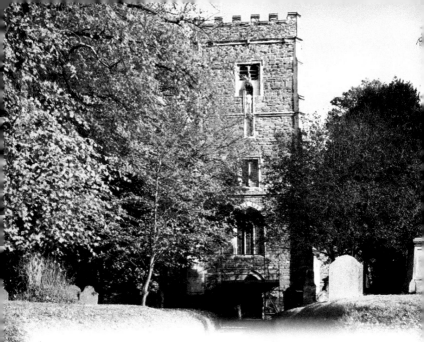

6. ST WOOLOS AND THE CATHEDRAL

St Woolos is a place of serenity and great history that stretches back to the fourth century. The early occupant of what was then a primitive tower was Gwynllyw, who was a warrior and, as folklore would suggest, a bit of a rascal. It is widely believed that Pillgwenlly, the name of the Newport Docklands district, originates from Gwynllyw. As every much-loved and respected rascal who resided in sight and sound of the sea will know, a man's boat is of primary importance to his wellbeing. The man in question moored his in Pill, which translated into English means 'Sea Ditch'. Therefore, the Sea Ditch belonging to Gwynllyw became Pillgwenlly.

However, that is not all this outstanding building has to say. A fine Norman arch is situated within, and the outward-facing statue high in the tower is missing a leg. This was removed by shot at the time of Oliver Cromwell, whose troops appeared to be destroying every cultural asset in the land at that time in our history.

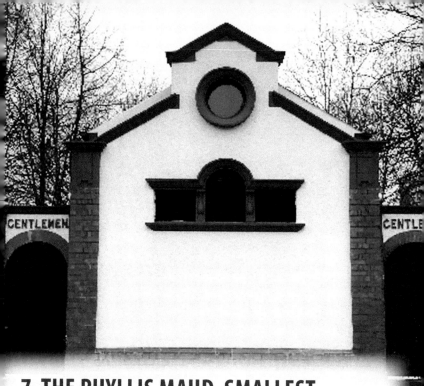

7. THE PHYLLIS MAUD, SMALLEST THEATRE IN TOWN

Hard to imagine how many folk have hung out around this neck of the woods. Victorian to the core, known by thousands, this toilet block has stood the test of time. When it closed because of the modern-day malady of improper use, it was acquired after much ado by Jan Martin of the Barnabas Arts Centre, and converted into a tiny community theatre. Here in front of around thirty people they will entertain, sing, read and recite poetry – an amazing achievement. This is almost on the same spot as the Timothy Bobbins puppet theatre popular in Pill around a hundred years ago.

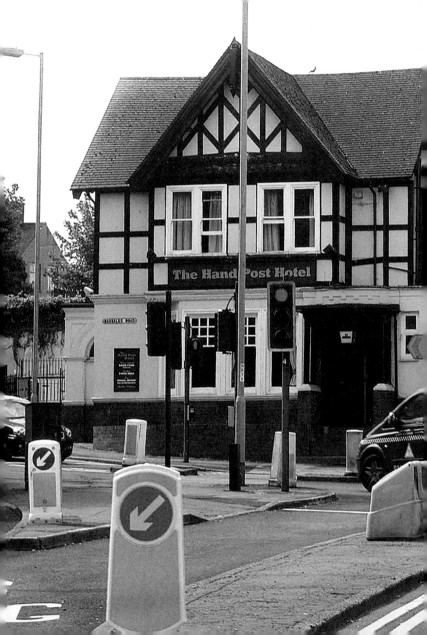

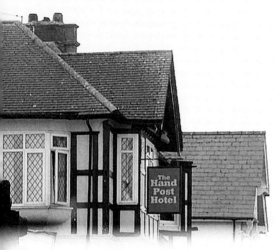

8. THE HAND POST

The idea of a hand post at this point was first discussed in 1842. It was to be a point from which visitors could be directed to their appropriate destination. Being at the junction of Risca and Basseleg Road, there were two defined directions. However the building as we know it was there in 1800, and was a lodging house for coach drivers making the arduous journey to and from the valleys on pitted roads and muddy tracks blighted with back-breaking potholes. The only other method of travel was the canal system to Crumlin.

The Hand Post must have been a popular watering hole for travelers. Leaving this point in 1800, those journeying to the Welsh valleys would have found themselves in open countryside quite soon. What an experience that must have been: the coaching horns, the pungent smells of sweat-drenched leather from the tackle suspended between the frantic, heavy horses, straining at their reins awaiting the crack of the whip and the inevitable command from the drivers.

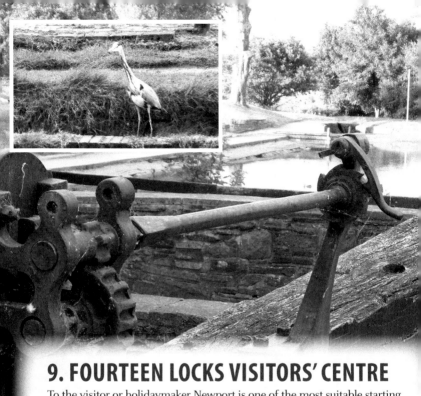

9. FOURTEEN LOCKS VISITORS' CENTRE

To the visitor or holidaymaker Newport is one of the most suitable starting points in the land. What makes it such is the short distance between the city centre and the open countryside. If it were a roulette wheel, all numbers would have a premium, for there are no routes out of the city that deny the traveller the delights of the countryside, the seaside or the mountains.

The resurgence of the canals in recent years has not gone unnoticed here in Newport and I believe at the time of writing long-term plans are being considered. A centre of learning and information has been built at Fourteen Locks. From here begins the long drag upwards and onwards to what was once the densely populated mining areas and the magnificent valleys. *Inset*: This spindly little fellow is one of the more recent visitors to the canalside.

10. BELLE VUE PARK

Newport can be justly proud of its flora and fauna. This beautiful park, set on a hillside adjacent to the main Newport to Cardiff road and until recently the Whitehead's steel plant, is Victorian. It is lush, secluded, and caters for many needs. The classic playground of slide, swings, roundabout and rocking horse has been superseded by a more modern style of play, in wood that has been profiled to the contours of the hill and includes walkways and safe areas of tree bark upon which children can land without harm – a far cry from years past when we went over the top of the swings, chewed pitch from the roof of the toilets and supped cold water from a public fountain!

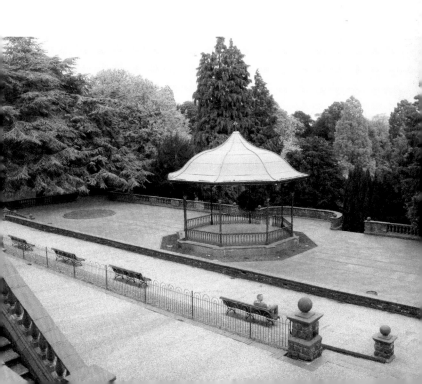

11. CARDIFF ROAD AND THE GATEWAY TO PILLGWENLLY

This is the Gateway to Pillgwenlly, and on this site stood the Salutation, the first pub built on what was marshland. It was also the first of numerous crossings of Commercial Road by the railway. Here the line split into two: one line ran just south of Dock Street station, and the other joined it at the town end. Whichever, the whole amalgamation proceeded next to the riverbank and the canal, to Cwmbran and all stations north, via Mill Street, Crindau and Malpas. In the day of the signalman, he would have been known as the bobby! Now there are more bobbies than one could shake a truncheon at, as the area is occupied by Newport's central police station. *Inset*: Commercial Road, the entrance to Pillgwenlly. Note the tramlines and overhead cables.

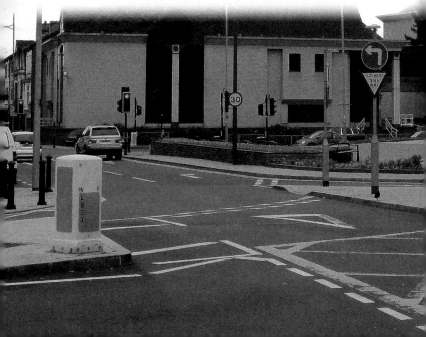

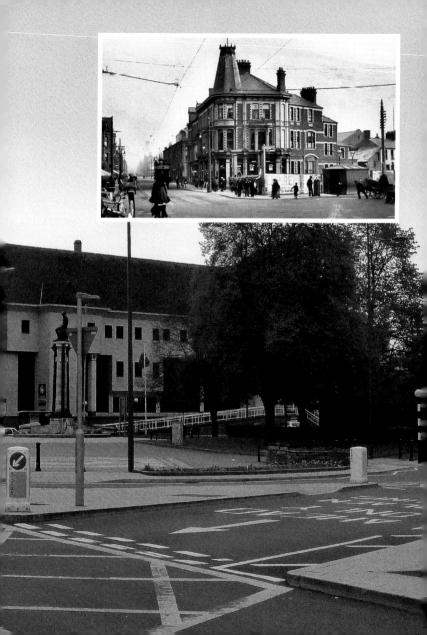

12. EARLY POWER TRANSFORMERS

An unusual aspect of Newport's industrial archaeology are the Park Square transformers. They date from 1894 when rubber-covered cable carried 2,000 volts, which was reduced to 200 for supplying the better-off households and larger homes in the area. The power station at that point was in Llanarth Street.

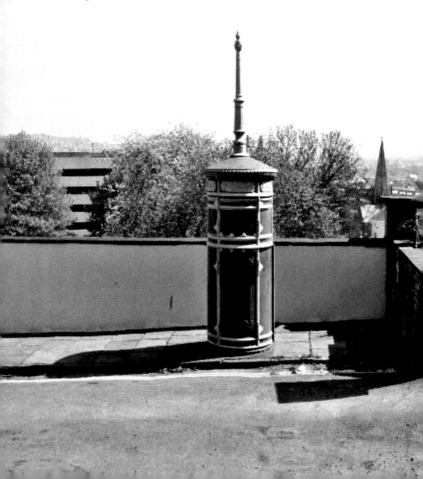

13. THE PARROT INN

The Parrot Inn was situated at the bottom of Hill Street. This spot has changed hands frequently; after the Parrot it was the Talbot and in recent times has been the home of The Body Shop and Woolworths, to name but three. It was however the Parrot that was once meeting rooms for the City Fathers up until 1835, until the rapidly expanding boundaries required more salubrious premises. It was also known as being the meeting place for the Newport Chartists of rioting fame; those who sat in the yellow glow of spitting tallow, shackled together by the common cause that led to the uprising.

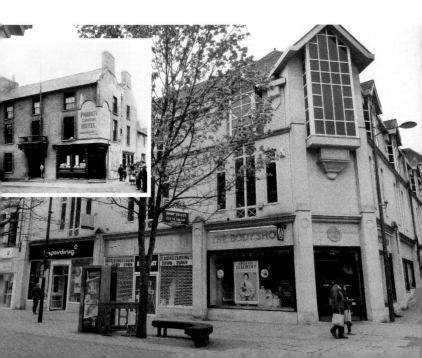

14. VICTORIA PLACE/PARK SQUARE

This is a most pleasant part of the city. Victoria Place, linking Stow Hill and Park Square, was built in 1844. In the 1970s it was completely refurbished and once again became a high-class street of Victorian town houses. Geographically elevated, it assumes a posture of superiority, and rightly so, for this delightful row has frequently been utilised by film and TV companies for period dramas. Here more than anywhere reflects how Newport really was in its heyday: a Victorian powerhouse for trade and industry.

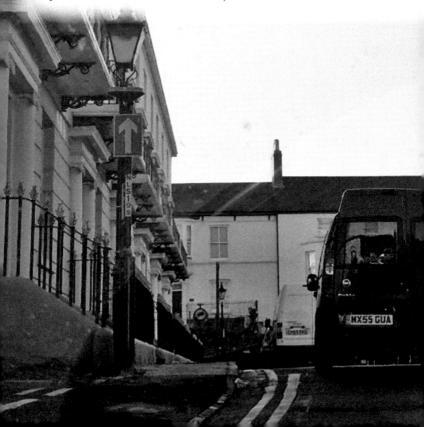

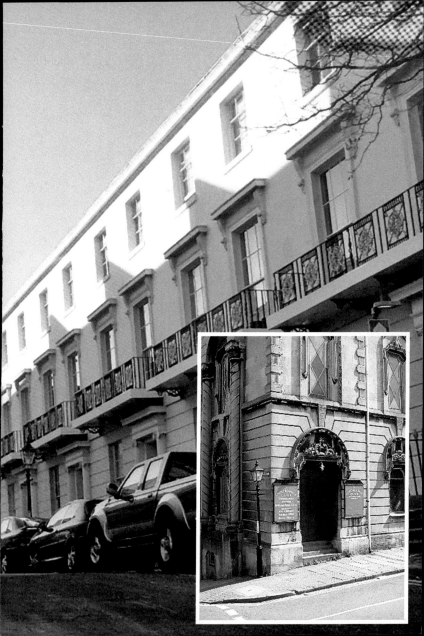

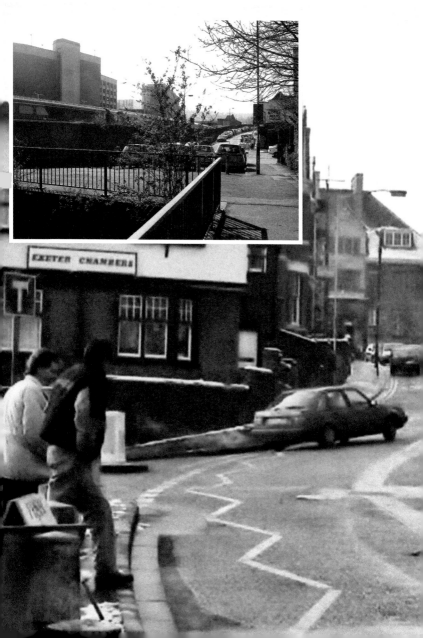

15. PENTONVILLE: ANCIENT VILLAGE OF PENDAN

The high-speed train accelerating out of Newport in the inset image is a far cry from the primitive oxen and cart of the past. Had you been in this spot in pre-Roman times, you would have undoubtedly been in the very heart of administrative life in Britain. The ancient British road, as opposed to the Roman variety, passed on this spot, meandering down over Christchurch Hill and into the watery levels via what is probably Church Road. One would have approached the ford, the river crossing where the current Newport Bridge is situated, entered a leafy cutting and arrived in Pendan, which is said to have been an important administrative centre for the island. Fishermen's Lane, leading to the fish store in Shaftesbury Street, would have pointed to the river crossing. 'Pentonville' comes from the name 'Pendan'. The densely populated area went into a slow decline as the Roman invasion created Caerleon, and when after 450 years they departed Britain, it sounded the death knell for the ancient British town.

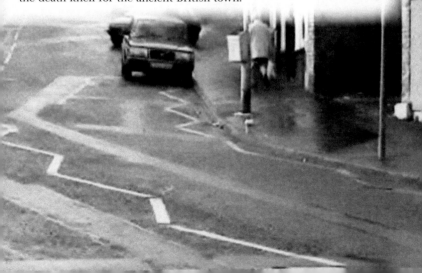

16. THE UNION INN

The Union Inn was built for the navvies who came each day at the break of dawn to manually hack out the soggy marshland to create a canal and then a large dock. The inn was lost many years ago, and standing afterwards were the Riverview Club and the Richmond Hotel. In the town itself there then existed the most vile and soulless lodging houses – so dire that they even lacked street names. From here the navvies came in a circuitous route across dangerous marshland, lacking roads and any form of lighting – their only guidance was the light that emanated from the Union Inn. They worked until dusk, walked the marshes to their place of rest and repeated the process again and again.

Inset: Lower Dock Street. The canal was situated to the right of the Octopus Bridge, looking toward the centre, which is where the photographer stood to take this 1970s image. At the time of building the canal none of this would have been in evidence.

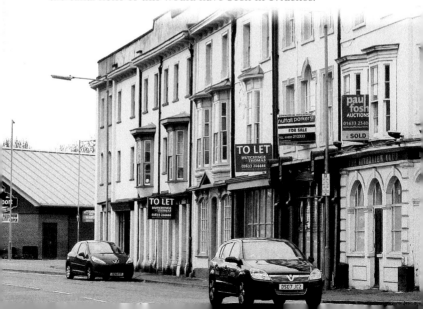

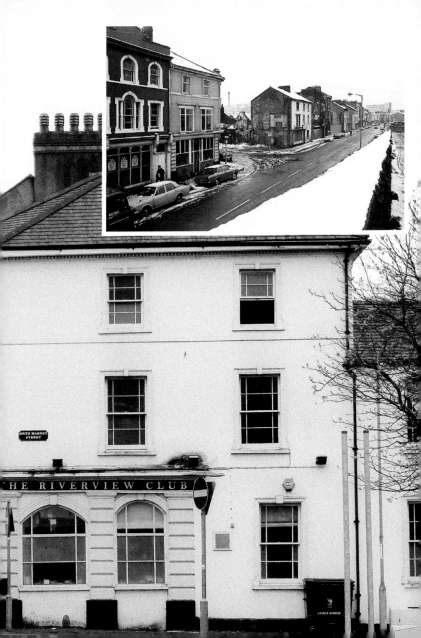

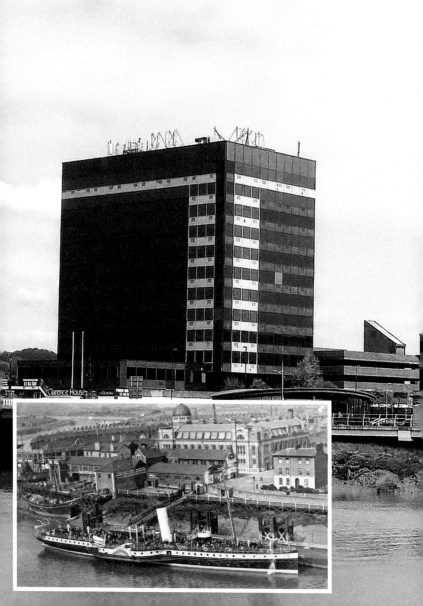

17. THE LANDING STAGE

To Holmes flat and steep, and to Barry and beyond. To cross the choppy Channel to rocky Ilfracombe, to celebrate Devon days of clotted cream and jam and scones. The pleasure steamers of P & A Campbell, laden with Newport people – men in the bar, ladies on deck enjoying the vapours of the power station and John Lysaght's Steel. Not long before the ozone takes over and the eggy wedges and cheddar cream crackers steal the limelight. Not long before the fizz of lemonade cries out in search of the taste buds of well-turned-out children itching to go down below to the bar, lined with heaven-sent bottles of orange and citrus bubbles. Not long before the said juveniles find the viewing platform in the engine rooms to gaze in wonder as the immense side paddles force the ancient flat-bottomed craft through the choppy waters of the Bristol Channel. It was the best bit.

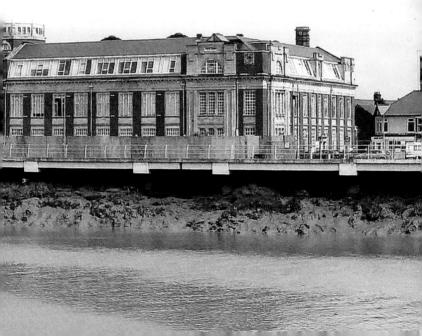

18. CASHMORE'S: THE GRAVEYARD OF LEVIATHANS

Perhaps Mariners' Graveyard would be more appropriate, for here the Leviathans of the ocean *Empress of France*, *Doric*, HMS *Gibraltar* and HMS *Collingwood*, late of the Battle of Jutland, gave out their final wisps of steam as they were carefully nudged onto the wharf walls of shipbreakers John Cashmore. There followed many other fine vessels of both the Royal Navy and the Merchant Navy services, one of which was HMS *Ajax* of River Plate fame. Badly mauled by the mighty *Admiral Graf Spee*, she drew her last breath on the banks of the River Usk here in Newport.

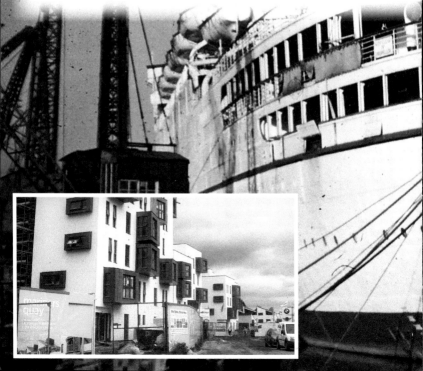

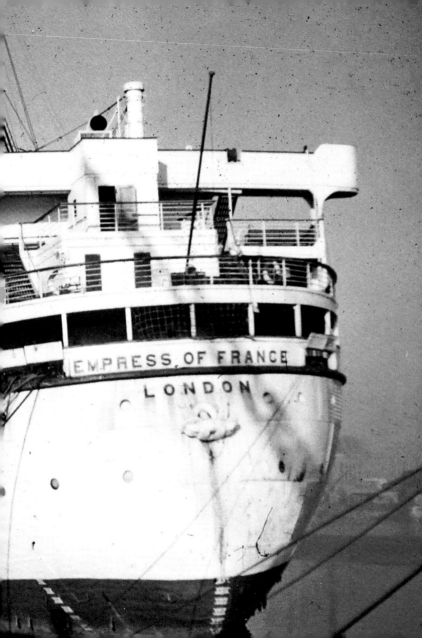

19. THE TREDEGAR DRY DOCK

Very little remains now of the Tredegar Dry Dock, bearing the name of its founder and the benefactor for much of Pillgwenlly. The dry dock was situated at the intersection of Alexandra Road and Commercial Road. The buildings which were emblazoned in the Tredegar name were pulled down just a few years ago. A new dual carriageway has disconnected it from the water; however, the imagery of a massive ship pointing directly up Commercial Road will never be forgotten. This was the visual effect it offered the traveller on the No. 9 omnibus en route to the docks.

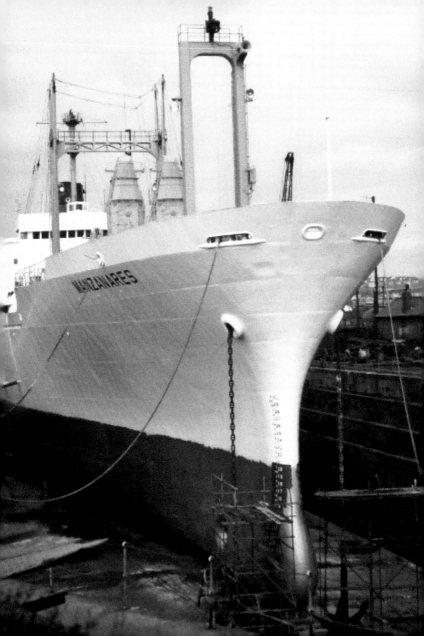

20. THE GAER ESTATE

The Gaer was an award-winning estate, one of the first in Newport to be built in a modern style, in the 1950s. It has always been a much sought-after area in which to live, perhaps because of the fine views across the Channel. This is particularly rewarding on a warm summer's evening, when the tide is high and the sky is clear. To the west side of the estate is the medieval Gaer Fort – difficult to see as it is covered in ferns and undergrowth, but nevertheless gives an insight into Newport's ancient past. *Inset*: Across the docks and the Channel from the Gaer.

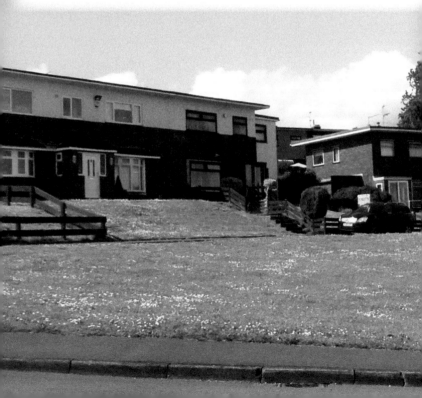

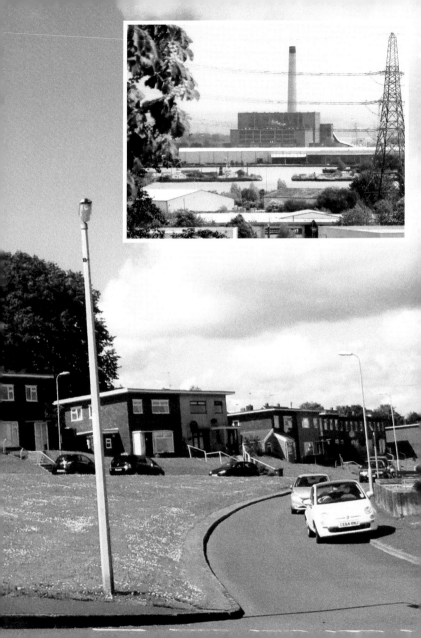

21. CHURCH HOUSE, W. H. DAVIES

William Henry Davies, Welsh poet and writer, spent much of his life abroad living as a vagrant. This building has been identified as his home. Standing forlornly amidst the desperation of redevelopment, it seems unfitting for such a famed scribe, who passed from this world in 1940. The building, which has become the Church House Inn, has clearly seen much refurbishment and it has been further suggested that the poet actually lived next door in a small terraced house, in the old street.

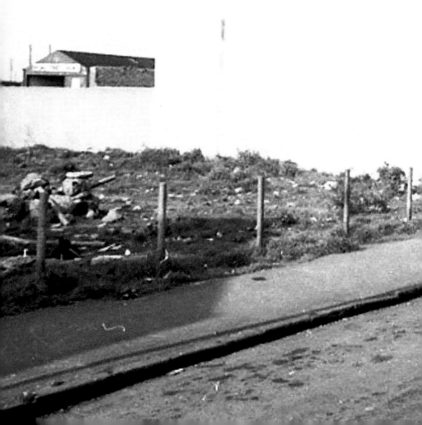

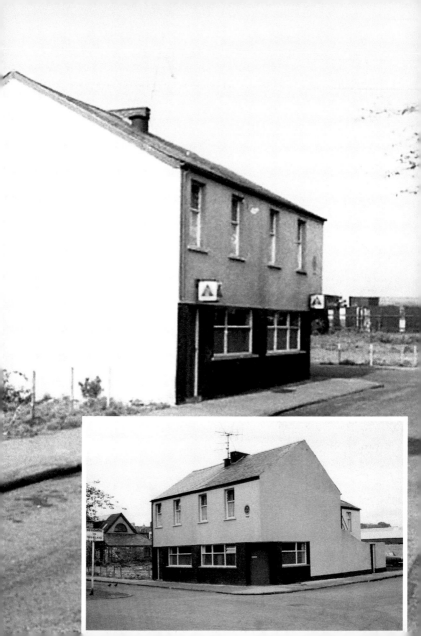

22. OLD POLICE STATION, PILL

Bring out your dead, lock up your drunks, extinguish the fire and if they don't survive the night, welcome to the mortuary. This incredible building once served as a police station to Pillgwenlly, as well as the fire station and the mortuary – a Victorian one-stop shop for all of life's displeasures. There was much going on in Temple Street. The mission to seamen occupied buildings near the junction with Commercial Road, the Pillgwenlly library was opposite until recently and the ragged school took a central position on the same side as the police station. In the late 1800s a tram road passed through the street as part of the intense dockland system of railways.

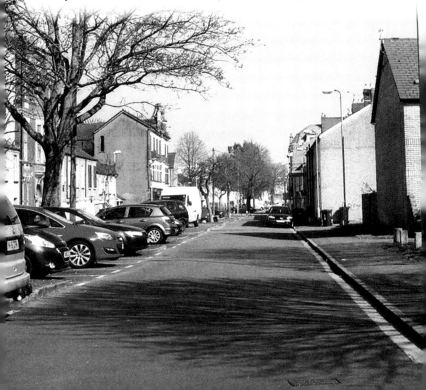

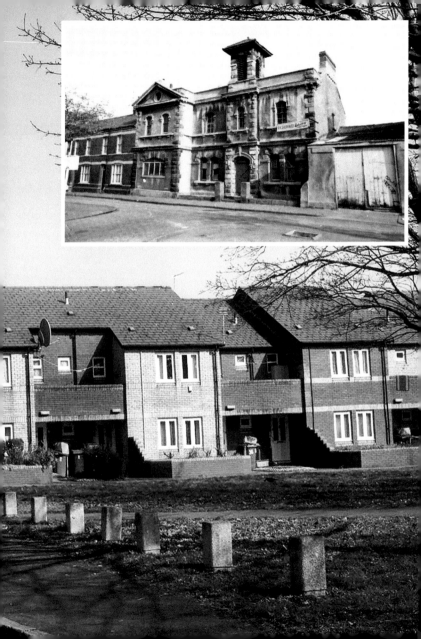

23. THE OLD TOWN HALL, HIGH STREET

Never has a building been so lamented as the old Town Hall. I suppose ownership makes it easy to declare something as not fit for purpose, or falling down, though it is widely agreed that pulling this fine building down was a travesty. Memories abounded and were steeped in the aged wooden wall panel – of romance, clandestine meetings on the steps, wartime dances and celebratory civic announcments. 'War is over', they screamed as the thronging crowds, jubilant with the sheer occasion, crammed the main street. Long live the king! Long live the Town Hall!

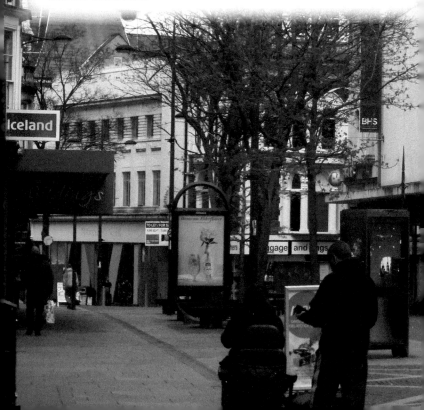

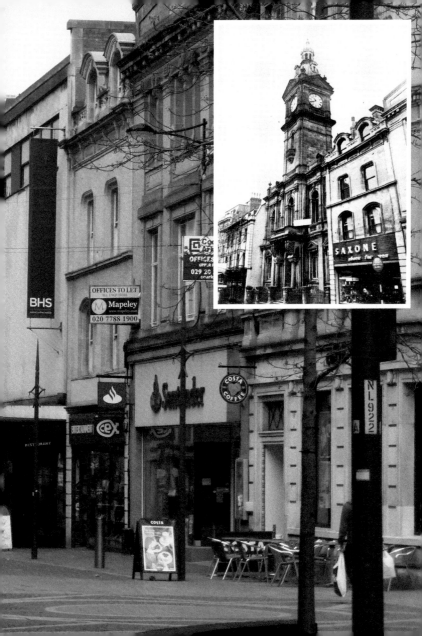

24. QUIET WOMAN'S ROW, ADJACENT TO THE OLD DOCK ENTRANCE

Quiet Woman's Row seems a strange-sounding name as we leave our vessels on the quayside and ponder our journey's end. Railway lines surround the twelve cottages like cupped hands offering the wanton soul to the Fisherman's Chapel of St James, which stands at right angles on the lock side. The coal hoists that separate the tiny cottages from the river's edge collect, lift and pour out their rich black cargoes of Welsh steam coal into the holds of the moored coaster or collier.

The ships' captains who once occupied this convenient waterside terrace have moved on to more salubrious climes. Three-story townhouses now stand in Pillgwenlly. Now it is us who stand in the row, the most dangerous and rowdy street in the town. This was not the case in 1812, when it was described as cosy, desirable and fashionable. Some fifty years later it had become grossly overcrowded, rowdy and uncontrollable. The name was derived from the Quiet Woman Inn, which showed a nun wearing a cowl on the sign. The nun looked like a headless woman, and as we all know, a headless person cannot speak!

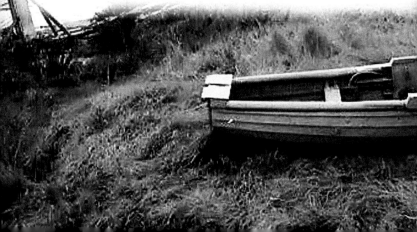

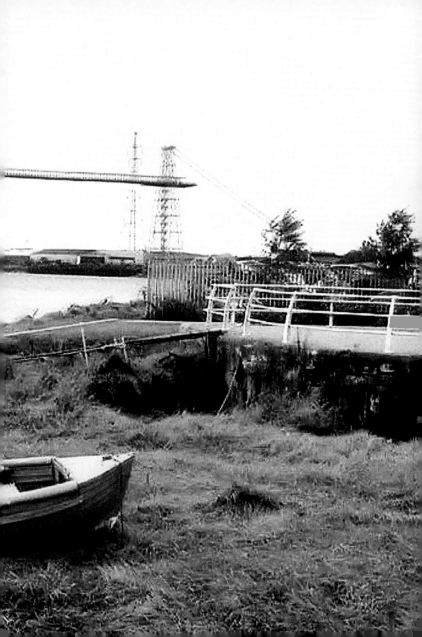

25. PILLGWENLLY: THE BEGINNINGS

It was inevitable that eventually there would appear a Tredegar Arms. Quite rightly so as there was a Tredegar Dry Dock, Tredegar Street, Tredegar Wharf School and the Tredegar Hall Cinema. Walk the length of this street, Church Street, and you will find a dual carriageway. Imagine the same without buildings, but for a few primitive cottages, and you would find the original hamlet of Pill – tumbledown dwellings next to a muddy mooring, constructed perhaps from ageing timbers and dry stone. A handful of small boats, fishing perhaps, but then came the Tredegar Dry Dock, the railway, Campbell's Pier and the houses. The rest is history.

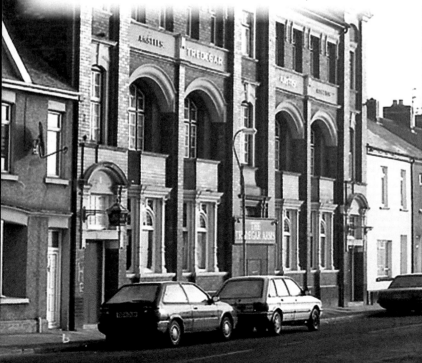

26. THE TRANSPORTER BRIDGE

Always a favourite, Newport communities have fought tooth and nail to keep this fine structure on the banks of the Usk in working order. It costs a fortune to maintain and has seen a number of major restoration and repair programs. It is still here, for which we must all be grateful. The bridge was opened in 1906 and was the work of the French engineer Arnodin.

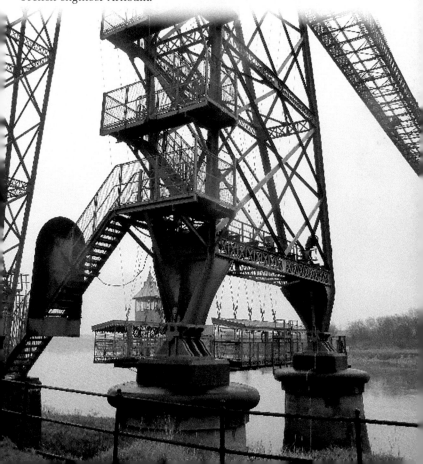

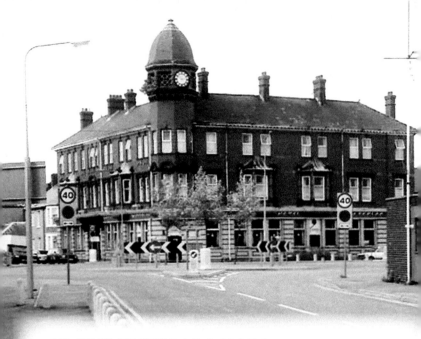

27. THE WATERLOO HOTEL

The Waterloo Hotel is probably Newport's most historic hotel. It is steeped in history and anecdote, from a time when dockers were paid out here, when the bar (said to be the longest in Britain) was so full you couldn't squeeze a cigarette packet between the throng of servicemen and seafarers lining it. This was in the war years, when it was said that the first sight of the famous clock tower would ensure one's safety from the evils of the U-boats, which would have followed the convoy into the Channel. The clock tower was once removed, but then rebuilt again. A fire caused much damage one Christmas, and the residents saved dozens of Christmas gifts stored for the local community party. In spite of the smoke and lack of electricity, the party went ahead as planned. This was in the days of Winston Boddy and his family, who ran the hotel for many years.

28. IRON GATES CROSSING

The little Great Western tank engines would slog their way up the incline to Cardiff Road and Courtybella, wind their way through the back streets of Pill and arrive here, one of the numerous crossings on Commercial Road by the maze of railway lines in Pill. Often the car driver would race the train to the gates as delays were frequent owing to the train movements. This was the neutral mile, a length of line that connected two railway companies, the Monmouthshire and the Great Western Railway. The line lasted for many years as a single track serving a coal distribution depot at Dock Street. *Inset*: As it is today.

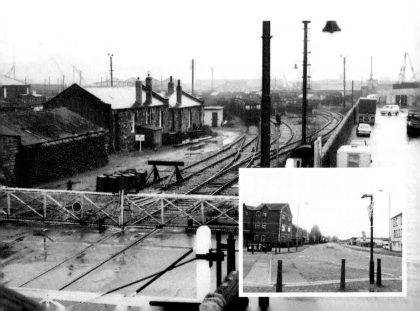

29. BARNABAS ARTS HOUSE, NEW RUPERRA STREET

Originally a mission church linked to St Paul's in Commercial Street, it was built on land purchased from Lord Tredegar and opened on 10 May 1906. It closed from lack of use in 1964 and was used for many years by Newport printing company the Central Press, who were also responsible for the production of the Newport County AFC matchday programme. In recent years it was obtained by Jan Martin, a progressive lady closely linked with fine arts. The church was reopened as an arts house offering work and display space and a performance area in a special and well-thought-out refurbished interior. Well worth a visit here for coffee and a browse.

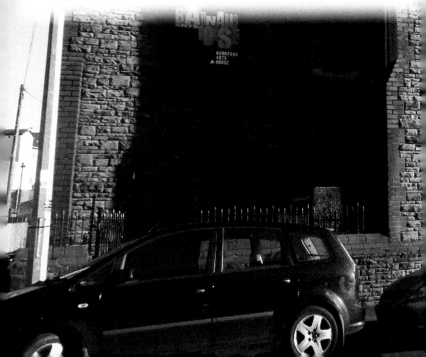

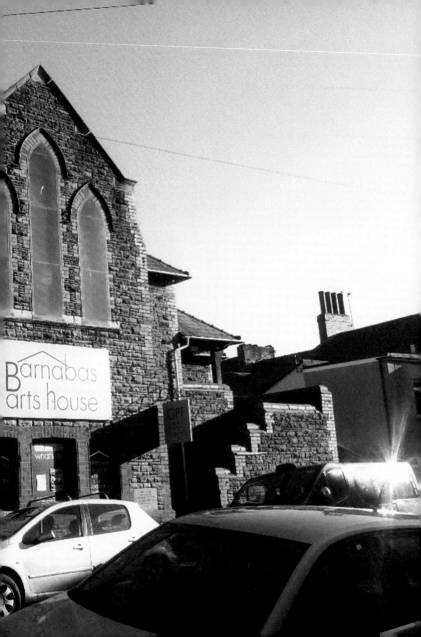

30. SEA WALL AT ST BRIDES/ THE LIGHTHOUSE

The emerald, weed-dressed reens are quite special. They help with flood management and farming and they contain fish. More to the point they are historic and have been here for hundreds of years. The actual lighthouse is now a private hotel but the area was once an attractive proposition for a cheap holiday day out within a few miles of the centre. The remains of a sea-fed swimming pool are still visible and rumour has it there was a small private menagerie here that kept monkeys. A day trip to the lighthouse was a common destination for horse-drawn charabanc outings from local pubs, clubs and societies. If nothing else it is bracing and a very nice walk towards Cardiff. *Inset*: The sea wall towards Cardiff.

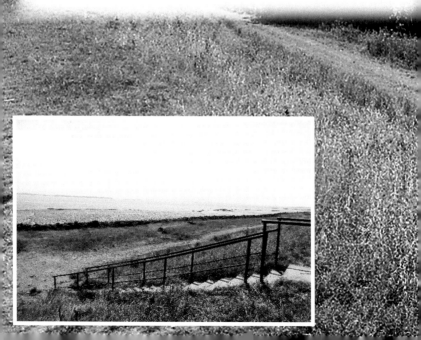

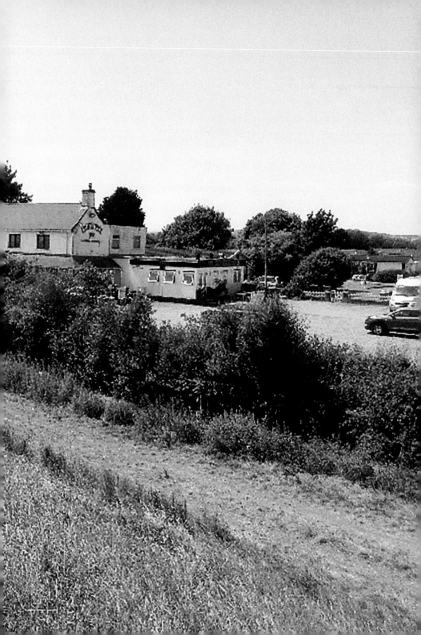

31. GOLDCLIFFE

In as much as Goldcliffe and the lighthouse are separated only by the river, Goldcliffe offers a different perspective and numerous views along the coastal path heading towards Chepstow and the Severn Bridge. Here also are the remains of the ancient salmon fisheries. There is substantial evidence of the Romans here, which at one point attracted the attention of the *Time Team* television programme. *Inset*: Ancient salmon fisheries.

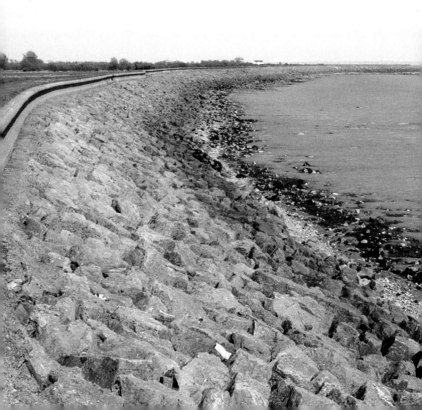

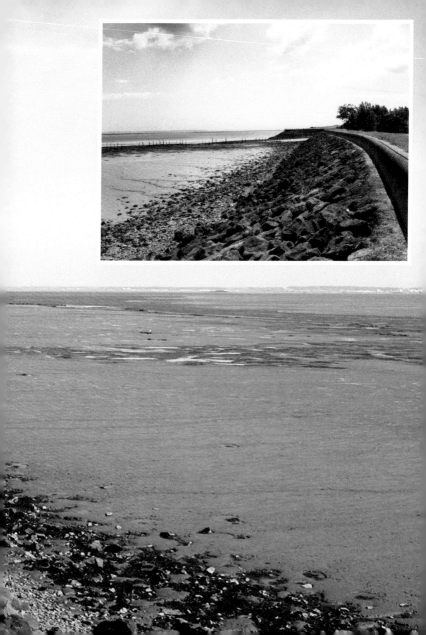

32. THE NEWPORT WETLANDS

There is something intensely pleasurable about spending time on the Gwent Levels. An intimate structure of life below knee level awaits the heavy-footed species of the human kind. Birds, waterfowl, frogs, toads, newts, grass snakes, eels and an abundance of fish are to be found in the maze of reens and ponds that lay just behind the shoreline.

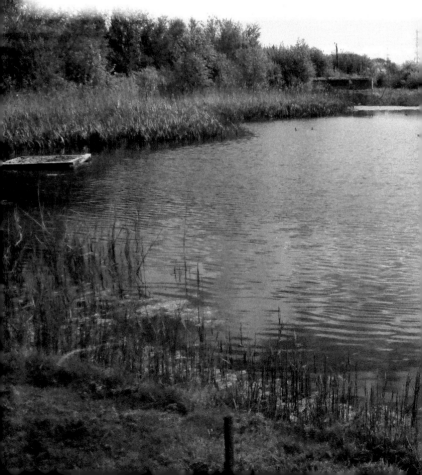

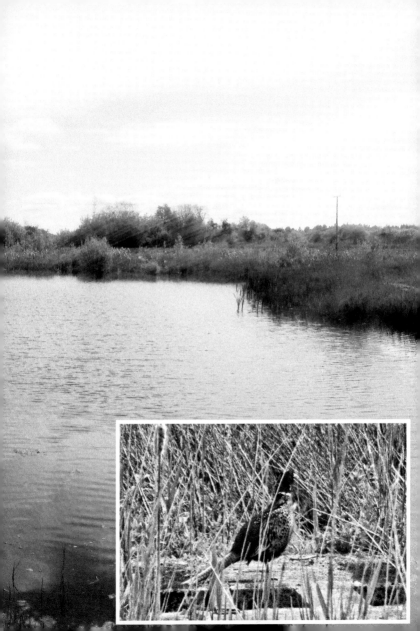

33. THE OLD GREEN, HIGH STREET

Such is the extent of the city centre development that it has proved impossible to mirror certain locations to images of the past. The Old Green is one case in point. A vast hole was created where the interchange used to be and all of the relevant history fell into it, never to be seen again. Once a part of High Street, this was in itself a golden thread in the commercial history of the town as it was then. The Corn Exchange, Fussell's, Wallace Jones and the National Fur Co. were just a few of the well-established names that once graced this extension to the main street. *Inset*: High Street before demolition.

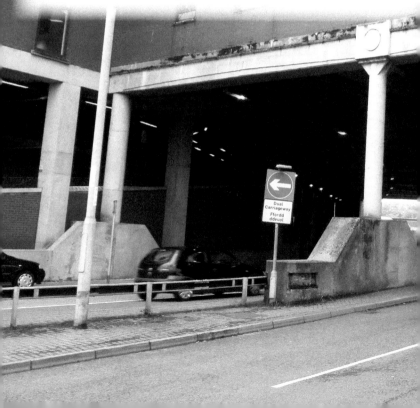

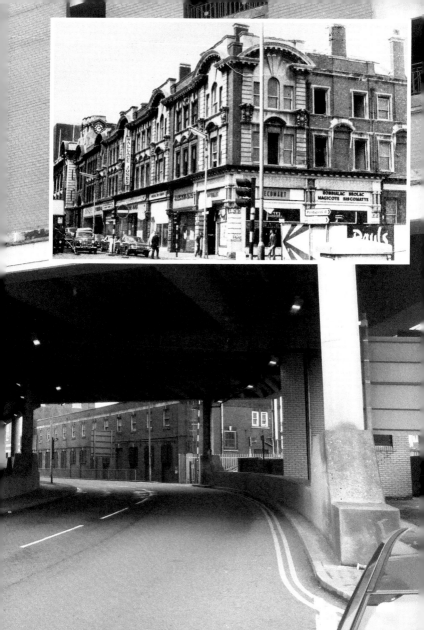

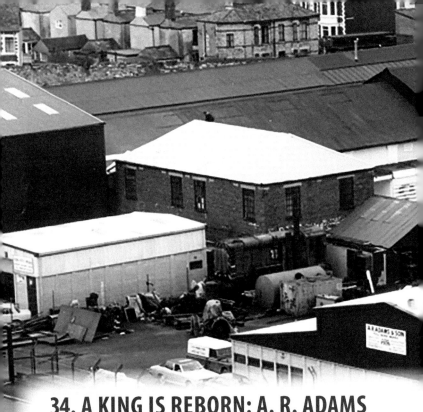

34. A KING IS REBORN: A. R. ADAMS

A. R. Adams, boiler makers and suppliers of industrial locomotives to the mining industry, was situated midway along Courtybella Terrace. They had a link to the docks branch of the then GWR, which in typical Newport style ran down the middle of the road. Their yard, which could be clearly seen from the iron footbridge across the railway line, was a potpourri of twisted metal, old cranes, boiler bits and a number of delectable old industrial steam shunting locos. It was a massive toy box. Pictured here is the last Adams yard in Pill, near the base of the transporter bridge. *Inset*: Beautifully restored by A. and R. Adams of Pill, Newport.

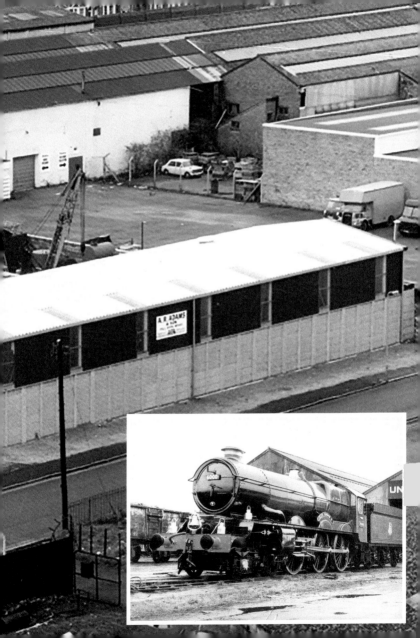

35. MUNITION CRECHE

This image shows the Munition Creche for First World War workers as it is today, as multi-occupation flats. Many tales of hardship come from this part of Newport on the edge of the Alexandra Dock, which perhaps is why the people of Pillgwenlly are so special to the city of Newport. *Inset*: Munitions workers, 1914.

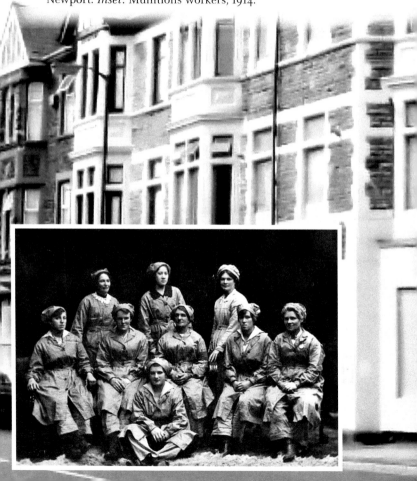

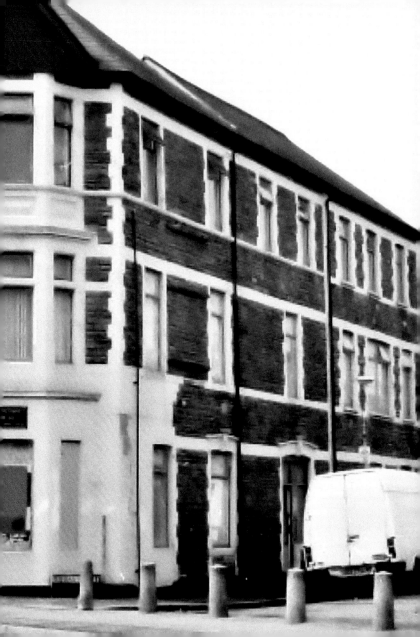

36. RIDGEWAY AND 'LITTLE' SWITZERLAND

Time spent here justifies much of what has been written about historic Newport. It's a two-for-the-price-of-one deal here, for on the left of the avenue the ground falls away steeply and a wide-ranging view is seen of what is often called Little Switzerland and the hill range to which Twmbarlwm belongs. Twmbarlwm is an ancient Silurian camp and it is said that between here and the barracks 100,000 men could be concealed. The ancient Britons are said to have made this their chosen site of government, in part because of the strategic advantages gained by hills, swamps and the river crossing. In addition to this, from this spot both eastern and western valleys can be seen, which in recent times were littered in mining and ironworks. With a little imagination you can see how modern Newport became so accessible for coal and minerals. To our right the view is of the city and a rather good eating house, The Ridgeway Inn.

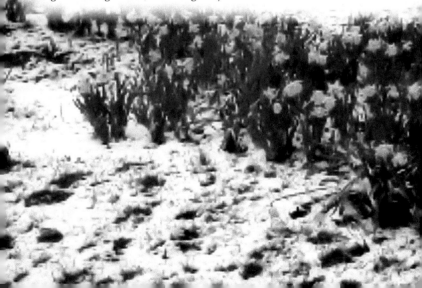

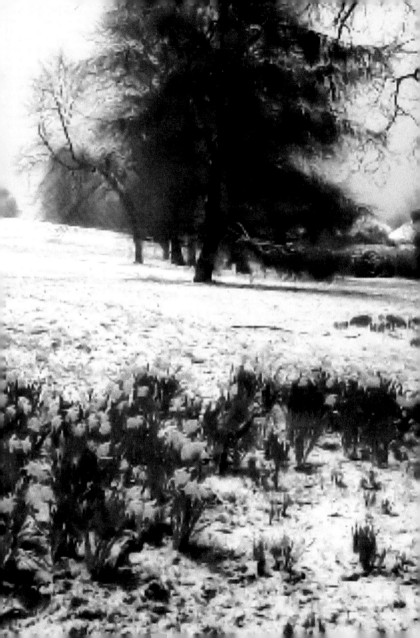

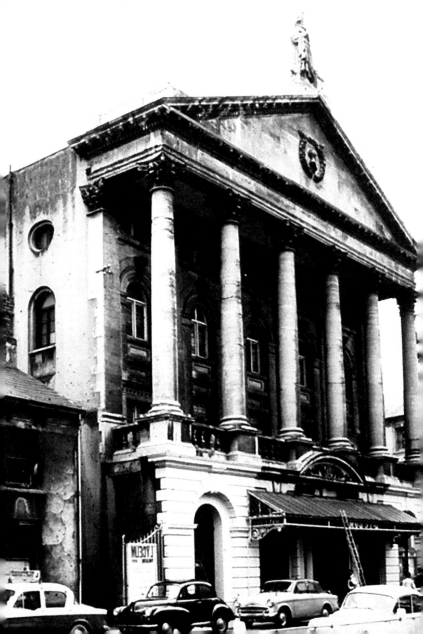

37. LYCEUM THEATRE, BRIDGE STREET

Another much-contested demolition was the magnificent Lyceum Theatre. On a par with the old Town Hall for style and elegance, with pillars and canopies over the entrance, it was what a city theatre was all about. Memories of the gods, the cheap seats high above the auditorium, and 'It's behind you!' Yes it certainly is now. An ABC Cinema was built on the site – oh dear, you can judge. The image below shows the site as it is today.

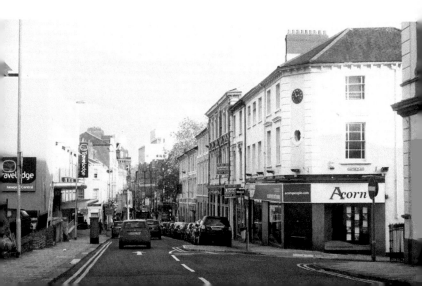

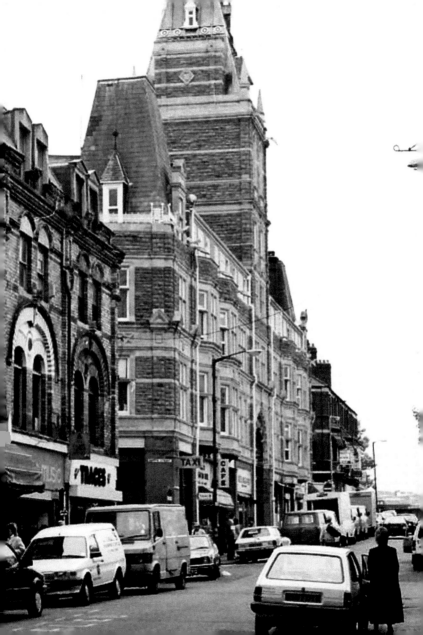

38. PROVISIONS MARKET

The provisions market was constructed on the site of the early canal basin and Pill. It is historically the place where Newport folk shopped. Each Friday and Saturday there was a pilgrimage to the market. Parking issues, redevelopment and modern shopping malls all played a hand in its struggle for survival. Nevertheless, traders are still there and it deserves support in whatever form it may take in the future. It is a beautiful Victorian palace of trade and commerce. The image below shows the original Newport Market House.

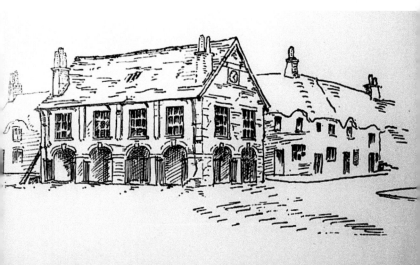

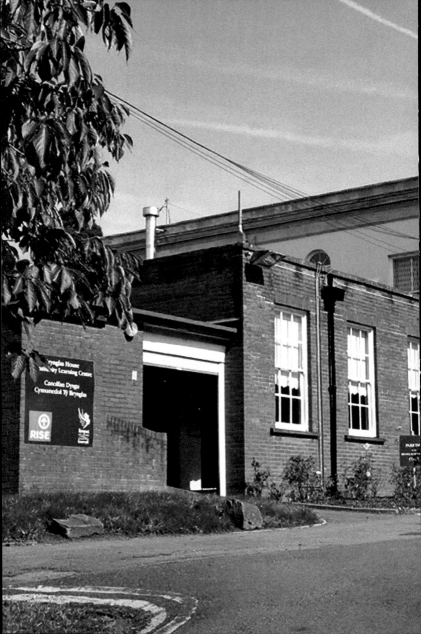

39. BRYNGLAS HOUSE

Even the red-brick addition doesn't look out of place on Brynglas House, which was once occupied by the Spanish industrialist James Cordes, who founded Newport's earliest works in the nineteenth century. It was later to become Brynglas Secondary School, when in the 1950s and early '60s the head still wore a cap and gown. Standing on the balcony outside his study, Acme Thunderer to his lips, any boy or girl arriving a minute beyond their time faced the cane or the dapper.

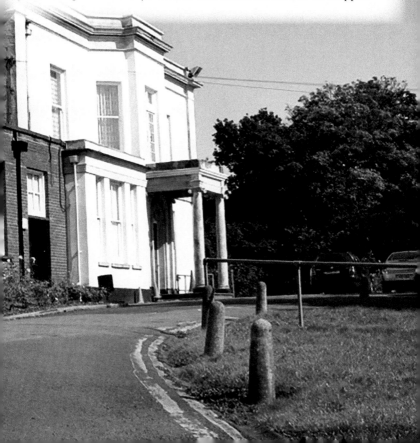

40. DOS WORKS

The Dos cottage still stands and is now the only evidence of Newport's first major works, the Dos Works, built in 1835 to manufacture nails and iron fixings of all types. Built by Spanish industrialist James Cordes, it was named the Dos Works as it was his second works – *dos* meaning 'two' in Spanish.

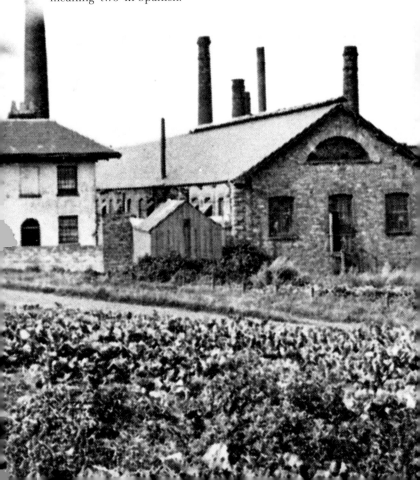

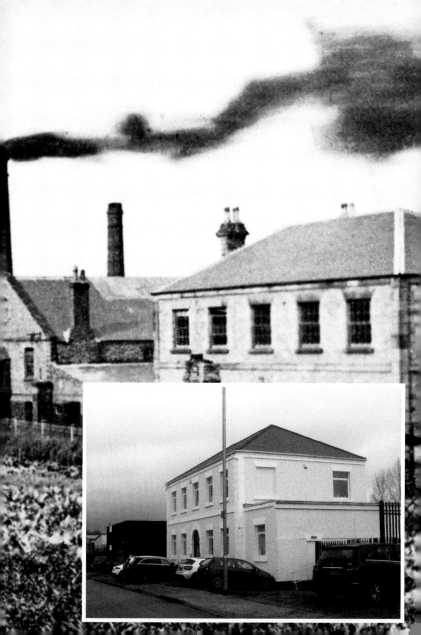

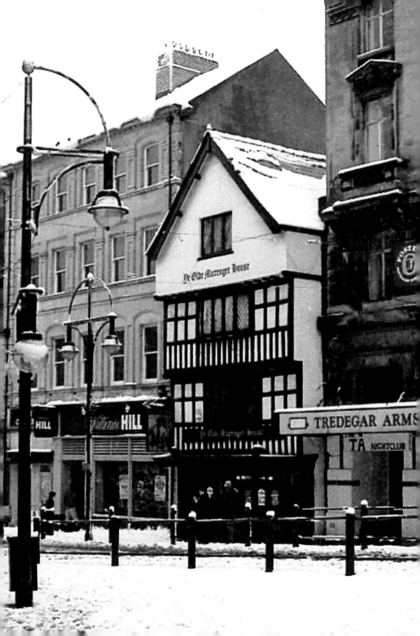

41. MURENGER HOUSE

Said to be the oldest building in Newport, the Murenger House dates from the mid-1500s. However a more realistic date would be the early 1700s, as this was probably a building on the site of the Murenger's House, or one which has been rebuilt, linked with the castle. The Murenger was the Keeper of the Keys, and that alone would justify a building being on the same spot many years ago when the castle was occupied.

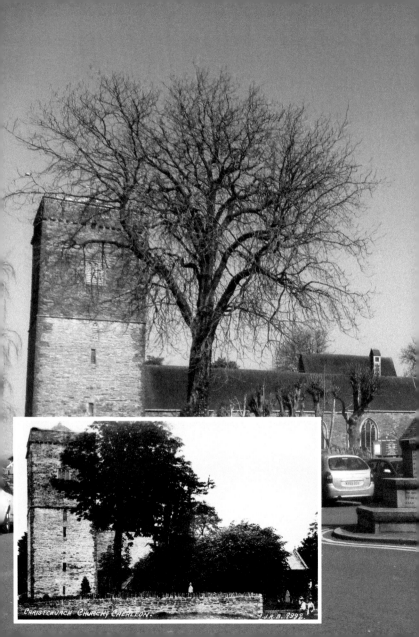

CHRISTCHURCH CHURCH, CAERLEON.   M.J.R.B. 1998.

42. CHRISTCHURCH

Holy Trinity Church in Christchurch village had an important visit some years ago. In 1648 during the English Civil War Cromwell's men decided to have a sleepover before attacking the castle at Newport. They obviously didn't enjoy the breakfast or their accommodation, for they smashed every window in the church – all but one, which is now safely preserved. More recently a cannonball of the period was discovered locally, adding more evidence to back up the event. Christchurch has history, but it also has amazing views of the Welsh mountains, the Channel and the lush Usk Valley. Membership to Cromwell's army is currently suspended.

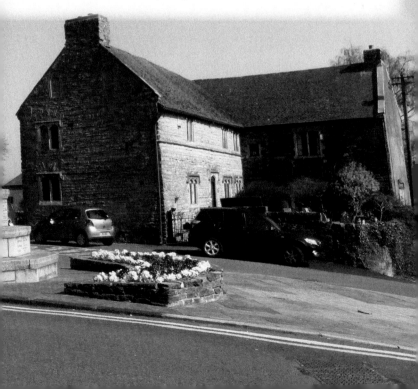

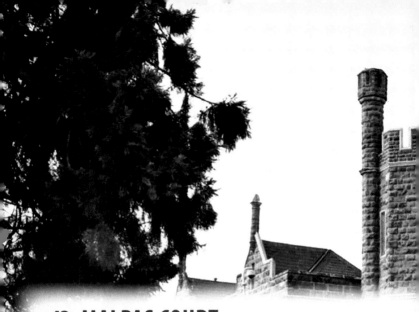

43. MALPAS COURT

Thomas Prothero once lived here, in the mansion (as the locals called it). Tomas Prothero could be cited as one of the fathers of the present city. The canal terminated at his wharf in Pillgwenlly. He sat on numerous groups and committees as an entrepreneur and industrialist. His name was associated with every major development in Victorian Newport. In the war years Malpas was an American camp that stretched to the canal. Nissen huts occupied most of the ground now called Malpas Court Estate. The remnants of the camp were still intact in the late 1950s and housed displaced people still finding their feet after the war years. A major outbreak of polio caused much panic and dismay to the other recently placed residents dragged from the 'slums' of Pillgwenlly and the like. (After six decades the definition of slum is still severely challenged.) The course of action taken by the youth of the 'court' was to hold their breath whilst passing the huts in case of airborne infection – not an easy task for five minutes.

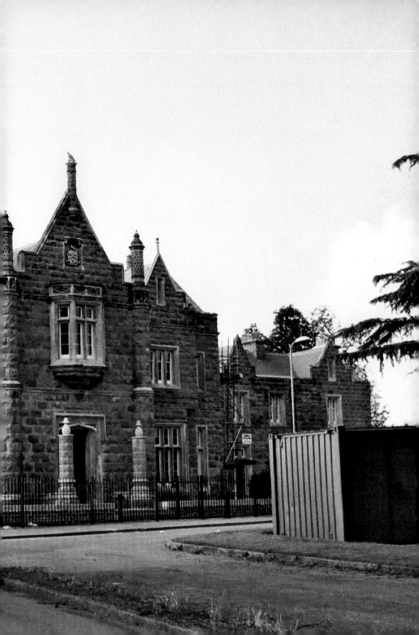

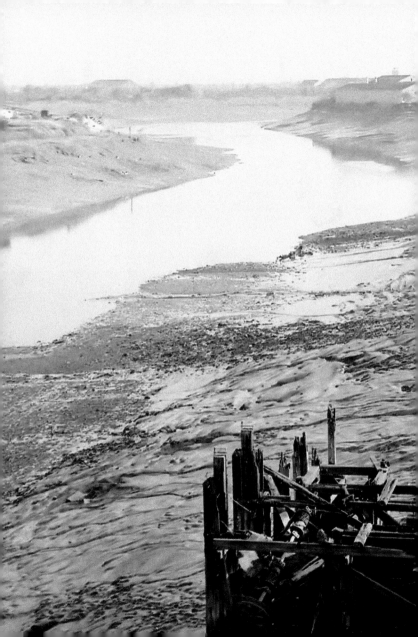

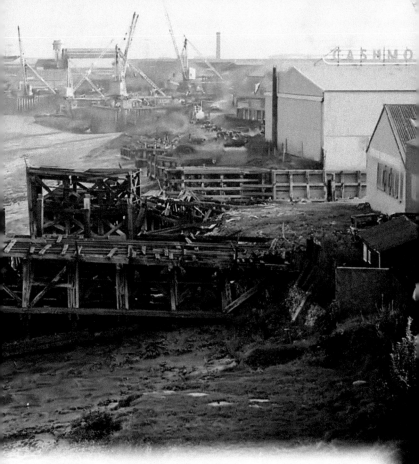

44. THE RIVER WHARVES

No more wharves on the river, at least not as we see here. This was the scene repeated from the docks to the town bridge; there were dozens of wharves, some stone, some timber. Small dockyards and shipbuilders catered for the needs of an absolute armada of shipping that called at Newport throughout the generations.

45. THE DOCKS

Grab a pie and a pint to fire the imagination and sit and listen to the history talking; from here it is telling a wonderful tale. The ships' masts and rigging might look like a spiderweb to the uneducated eye, yet every inch and every block and tackle was known intimately to the jack tar, whose task it was to present this mass of sailcloth and rope to the prevailing sou'wester as the laden craft headed into the Severn. Listen to the sounds of the Victorian docklands, a beautiful melody of iron-clad cartwheels clattering over the cobbles, the cuss of the man with the obstinate mule, the omnipresent throb of steam hammer and press as the full volume of the Industrial Revolution spreads like wildfire through stone-walled warehouses and terraced streets. The drag of the chain as, link by link, great anchors rise from the silt- and coal-thickened mud of the estuarial Usk. This was the Old Town Dock.

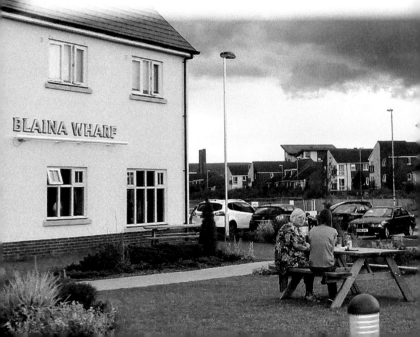

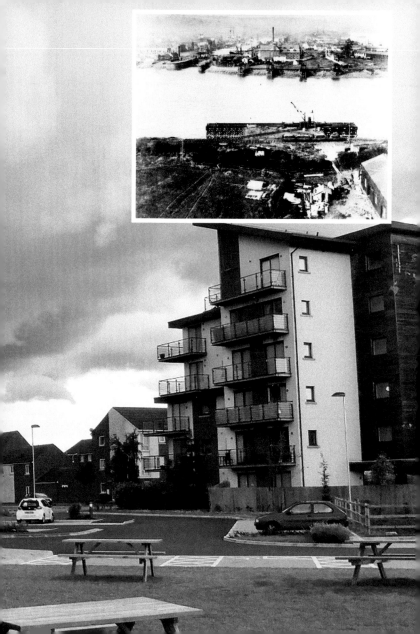

46. ALEXANDRA DOCK

Walking to the pier head was a regular Sunday occurrence; a few miles on a Sunday afternoon twixt roast and trifle with bread and butter cleansed the soul and the palette. Nowadays, entrance to the dock is no longer allowed. However, the view from most elevated positions in the west of Newport will give you a glimpse of the pier head and docks area.

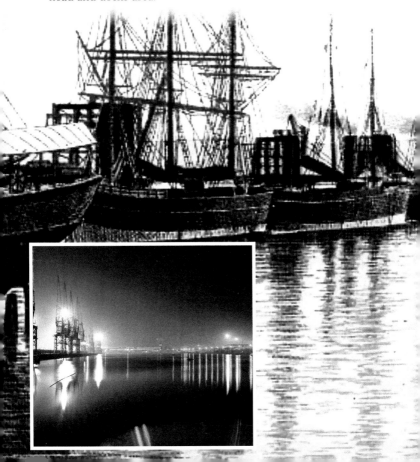

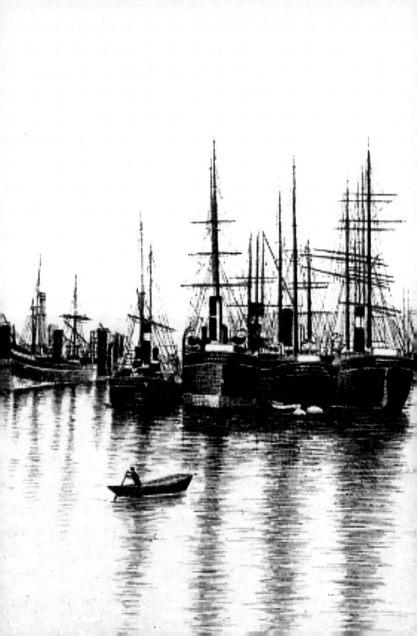

47. THE USKSIDE ENGINEERING COMPANY

On a winding engine so far away it says, 'Made by the Uskside Engineering Company, Newport Monmouthshire England'. The company was formed in 1827 and anchors and massive chains were forged in the works. In 1852 it was bought by John Hughes and became an ironworks. Hughes moved to the Midlands and then emigrated to Russia, taking over seventy Welsh workers and families, where he started the New Russian Company, an ironworks that lasted for many years after his death. Another interesting aside is the story of how the company, when in need of extra space, bought half a street from Newport Corporation. This was Speedwell Street, which until recently still existed within the confines of the works.

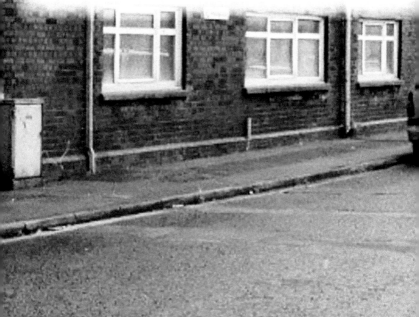

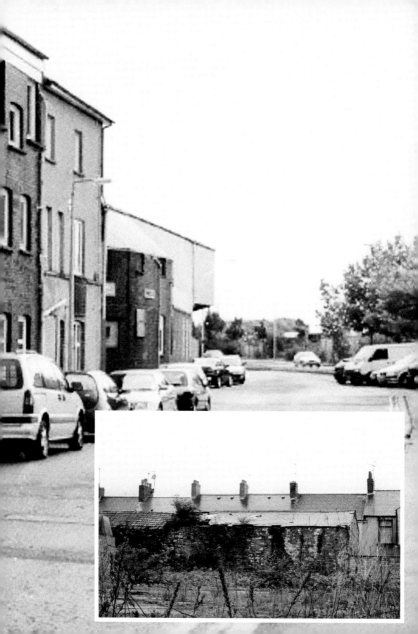

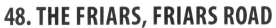

48. THE FRIARS, FRIARS ROAD

Originally this was a religious house for the White Friars of the Carmelite Order, but as with many other examples of architecture, it was altered and eventually was the residence of Thomas Prothero, who also occupied Malpas Court at one stage. Now it belongs to the Glan Hafren Trust and is part of the hospital system.

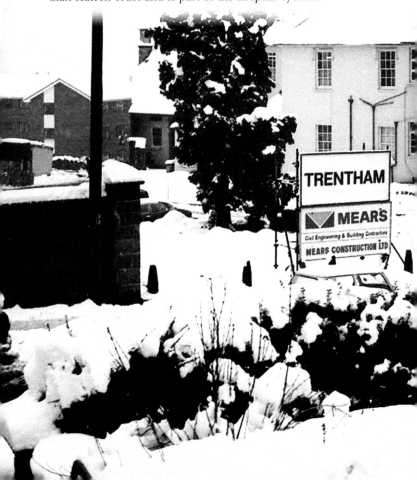

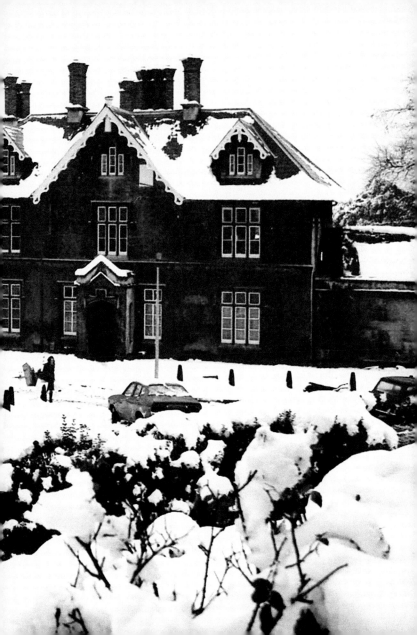

49. THE CATTLE MARKET

A spacious cattle market was constructed and enjoyed by the town in 1844. It was a substantial site and could hold 1,000 pigs, 2,000 sheep and a cattle shed of 350 ft x 23 ft, a horse shed and also two sheds for the sale of wool and agricultural machinery. It was constructed by the Tredegar Wharf Co., prompted by Charles Morgan, and the construction work was supervised by Samuel Homfray – three individuals synonymous with the creation of Newport as it stands today. The cattle market was closed in recent years and is now occupied by Asda. The cattle sheds have however been preserved as listed buildings.

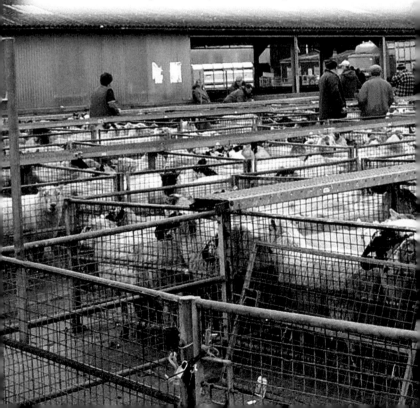

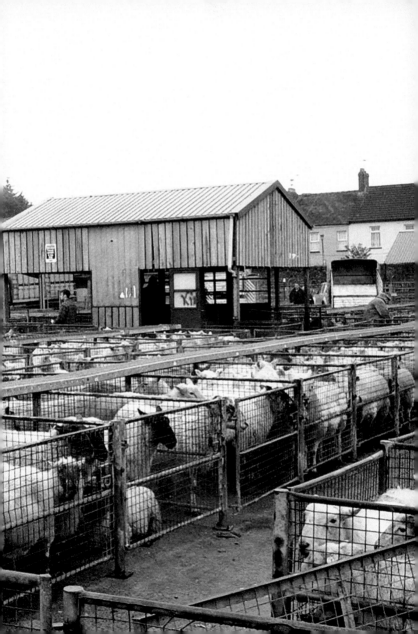

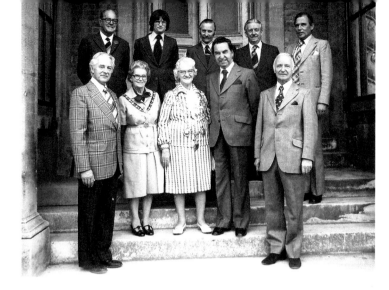

50. TREDEGAR HOUSE
AND COUNTRY PARK

In the late 1970s Newport acquired this country estate, which was for 500 years the home of the Morgans, who became the Lords Tredegar. This large sprawling country estate has now been transferred to the National Trust. It has many fine architectural features, and provides a wide range of activities. The picture above was taken during the first Newport Country Show held at the estate, and includes the Right Hon. Roy Hughes MP and members of Newport Council and show organisers.

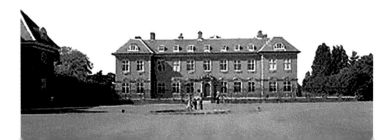